How We Came to Stand on That Shore

How We Came to Stand on That Shore

Jay Rogoff

THE RIVER CITY POETRY SERIES
RIVER CITY PUBLISHING
MONTGOMERY, ALABAMA

©2003 by Jay Rogoff.
Published in the United States by River City Publishing,
1719 Mulberry Street, Montgomery, AL 36106.

All rights reserved under International and Pan-American Copyright Conventions. No part of this publication may be reproduced, stored in a retrieval system, or transmitted in any form or by any means electronic, mechanical, photocopying, recording, or otherwise, without the prior written permission of the publisher.

Printed in the United States.
Designed by Nancy Stevens.
Cover Art by Ignacio Iturria,
detail from *Los Inmigrantes*, oil on canvas, 1990.

Library of Congress Cataloging-in-Publication Data:

Rogoff, Jay.
How we came to stand on that shore : poems / by Jay Rogoff.
p. cm. -- (River City poetry series)
ISBN 1-57966-032-0
I. Title. II. Series.

PS3568.O486H69 2003
811'.54--dc21
2002154528

For Diane, Herb, and Leslie

Contents

Acknowledgments   8

How We Came to Stand on That Shore
Seltzer   12
Visions of Great-Grandmother   15
Documentary   17
Welcome to the Family   20
The Trophy   23
My Grandmother in the Home   25
Behind the Door   26
Did the Black and White Movies Make My Mother?   27
Grandma's Cooking   29
My Mother's Studio Apartment   34
The Planes Came Home to the Airport   35
How We Came to Stand on That Shore   37
Good Night   39

Transportations
Teaching My Students Prosody   42
Playing Ariel   45
The Rock and Roll Angel   46
The Invention of English   48
George Herbert   50
Redon Discovers Color   52
Paley Park, East 53rd Street   54
Hogan's Bar, Galway   55
Inishmore Cuckoo   56
In the Lake   57

First Hand

From asphalt to dirt road to muck 62
A quart of milk weighs two pounds. A gallon weighs 63
Unless I go down town to get it stretched, 66
At night the cows sleep on the hill, 67
She comes into the barn to say hello, 68
Labor is neither blossoming nor dancing. 69
To break open earth for the sake 70
Although we live under one roof, my cloak 71
Here things get repaired in tumult: the clang 72
Solstice 73
St. Swithin's Day 74
"Deny the plow that furrows land. Division," 76
Although I have stolen his golden girl, 77
Harvest 78

Scattering Bright

Strown Bliss, Scattering Bright 80
Toll Road, Winter 81
Three Sisters, Late Summer 82
Ritual 85
The Vintage 86
Returning 87
Awakening 88
A Ghost 89
Redemption 91
A Woman Wades into the Sea 93
Driving in Fog 95

Acknowledgments

The author gratefully acknowledges the publications in which the following poems first appeared, many of them in different form: "Paley Park, East 53rd Street" and "The Trophy" in *Asheville Poetry Review*; "The Invention of English" in *The Hudson Review*; "Behind the Door" in *Many Waters*; "A Ghost," "My Grandmother in the Home," and "Toll Road, Winter" in *Metroland*; "Visions of Great-Grandmother" in *MSS*; "Strown Bliss, Scattering Bright" in *The New Republic*; "Documentary" and "In the Lake" in *Poetry Northwest*; "Driving in Fog," "Seltzer," and "Three Sisters, Late Summer" in *Present Tense*; "How We Came to Stand on That Shore" in *The Quarterly*; "Ritual" and "The Rock and Roll Angel" in *Salmagundi*; "Good Night" and "My Mother's Studio Apartment" in *The Tennessee Quarterly*; "Did the Black and White Movies Make My Mother?" in *The Yale Review*; and "George Herbert," "The Planes Came Home to the Airport," "Playing Ariel," and "A Woman Wades into the Sea" in *Zone 3*.

"Teaching My Students Prosody" originally appeared in *The Georgia Review*, volume 38, number 2 (Summer 1984). Copyright 1984 by the University of Georgia. Reprinted by permission of *The Georgia Review* and Jay Rogoff.

"Redon Discovers Color" first appeared in *Partisan Review*, volume 52, number 4 (1985). Copyright 1985 by Jay Rogoff.

"Hogan's Bar, Galway" and "Inishmore Cuckoo" are reprinted from *Prairie Schooner*, volume 60, number 4; "Welcome to the Family" from volume 68, number 3; and "Grandma's Cooking" from volume 71, number 1, all by permission of the University of Nebraska Press. Copyright 1986, 1994, and 1997 by the University of Nebraska Press.

"Awakening" and "The Vintage" (as "Vintage") were first published in *The Sewanee Review*, volume 104, number 4 (Fall 1996). Copyright 1996 by Jay Rogoff.

First Hand won the Poetry Society of America's John Masefield Memorial Award for narrative poetry and appeared as a chapbook from Mica Press. It was first published in its entirety, in slightly different form, in *The Poetry Society of America Bulletin*. Four of its sections first appeared in *Kansas Quarterly* as "Aubade in Spring," "Harvest," "St. Swithin's Day," and "Solstice"; one section in *The Minnesota Review* as "Labor"; and one section in *Yet Another Small Magazine* as "Ploughing." One section originally appeared as "The Wedding Sermon," reprinted from *Prairie Schooner*, volume 60, number 4, by permission of the University of Nebraska Press. Copyright 1986 by the University of Nebraska Press.

"Teaching My Students Prosody" was reprinted in *The Georgia Review*'s Fortieth Anniversary Poetry Retrospective issue and in the subsequent anthology *Keener Sounds*; "Paley Park, East 53rd Street" in *CityLegacy;* "Seltzer" in *Library Bound: A Saratoga Anthology;* "Grandma's Cooking" in *The* Prairie Schooner *Anthology of Contemporary Jewish American Writing*; and "How We Came to Stand on That Shore" in *Cabin Fever: Poets at Joaquin Miller's Cabin, 1984-2001; Library Bound: A Saratoga Anthology;* and *Split Verse.*

The excerpt from "The Player Piano," from *Complete Poems* by Randall Jarrell, is copyright 1969, renewed 1997 by Mary von S. Jarrell, and reprinted by permission of Farrar, Straus and Giroux, LLC.

The excerpt from *Old Times* by Harold Pinter is copyright 1971 by H. Pinter Ltd. and reprinted by permission of Grove/Atlantic, Inc.

I am grateful to the MacDowell Colony and the Corporation of Yaddo for residencies during which some of these poems found their final form.

I owe special thanks to Ignacio Iturria for permission to use his wonderful painting *Los Inmigrantes* on the cover. My thanks also go to Ignacio's agent, Pablo Iturria, for his assistance, and to Christopher Gonzales and Jennifer Jolly for their generous help in translating our correspondence.

For encouragement and advice about many of these poems I am most lucky to have had the guidance of Philip Booth, Andrew Hudgins, Penny Jolly, B. D. Love, Katha Pollitt, and the late and much-missed M. L. Rosenthal.

How We Came to Stand on That Shore

There are some things one remembers even though they may never have happened. There are things I remember which may never have happened but as I recall them they take place.

–Anna in Harold Pinter's *Old Times*

Here are Mother and Father in a photograph,
Father's holding me. . . . They both look so young.
I'm so much older than they are. Look at them,
Two babies with their baby. I don't blame you,
You weren't old enough to know any better. . . .

–Randall Jarrell, "The Player Piano"

Seltzer

In a glass between my hands I hold the past:
not a trickling through a choked glass neck
but a deeper bubbling up
like used breath: clear, stony, bitter. All things

come back: seltzer—in polystyrene liters
whose screw-caps spray crazily round the kitchen,
a clear descent from the magisterial
blue-glass siphon that advertised *Good Health*,

presiding on my grandparents' tablecloth
squat, serene, mysterious as Buddha.
Weekly my hands would blacken with rubbing
Dick Tracy's pointy jaw in the comics

of the exotic Sunday *News*, as Zaydee
would stub his Camel out, slick back his hair
with yellow fingers, and produce the bottle
of yellower pineapple syrup. He'd pour

an unbearably slow dollop
into a tumbler sculpted like shul windows,
which I'd hold to the gleaming spout. I'd squeeze
the siphon's trigger—*sploosh!*—and transfigure

the rainy day by effervescence, so
the old light arriving through thickening
slabs of kitchen window, stuttering
through dust-scented lace curtains, would never

fade to dark. The seltzer-bubbles prickle
my nostrils like my pineapple schpritz's,
gushed from the siphon, its bottled power
threatening to burst: the charge of the Czar's

horses' hooves beneath the Russian sun springing
off swords, the trundling of bundles miles
and miles to port. Then huddled in steerage,
my grandmother creeping out, four, seasick,

begging the captain's scraps for her mother,
who ten years later locked in fury the door
against my grandfather, poor, apprenticed
to a tailor, affecting tailor's black.

One day when her mother had gone to market
he took those slender fingers in his callused ones.
They look out through the yet-unwavering glass
at a continent to conquer, a shining sky

(New Lots Avenue, where boys in payis
and black fur-felt hats belt a stickball,
their ears opened to the stubborn thunder
of the el's cattle-cars overhead),

and they stare together at the siphon
with all its bottled trouble, on the table
standing blue and solid as all time.
My grandfather shoots a jet into a tumbler.

He sips, gulps, and hands the glass to her.
All of fifteen, he asks her hand in marriage.
She stares, all of fourteen, into the glass,
sips, swallows, and turns to present her face to him.

Visions of Great-Grandmother

Grandmother kept the photo of her mother
on her nightstand until the day she died,
as if it could dictate her every move.

Sometimes it did. Unflappable, fox-nervy,
my four-foot-ten grandmother, who once shamed
three giant muggers into running off,

recoiled into a childish helplessness
before the picture in its tarnished frame
weighty with silver fruit. "Mom, she's dead

ten years," my father would explode. "Do what
you like!" Yet who would dare to disobey
the face resplendent above that high starched collar,

the eyes gray and clear, excavating secrets?
Her nimbus of hair hid a mind like lightning;
her mouth exacting as the wide horizon

brought heaven to the full earth lip to lip.
I imagine Minsk as Byzantine, gold
mosaic domes, and spires, and minarets.

Fingers twangling on their balalaikas,
the goyim whistle folksongs in the streets,
needling my great-grandmother as she sings

a keen countermelody. In the cold
darkening house from her silver ladle
soup steams. Tonight we all can eat till full.

Across from me my grandmother's eyes glimmer
nocturnally, four years old. Out the window
shadows crawl as great-grandmother breaks bread.

Under her Nefertiti wrappings
and ritual corsets dormant fires flicker.
My grandmother's eyes widen. So do mine.

Since dawn I've had my woolens bundled with
my Chumesh. Now we scrub each dish. Who knows
if we'll discover clean where we are headed?

The boat will have an orchestra, and marble
decks, and ices carved into ten-story
skyscrapers, and seven of every clean

animal. We will follow her anywhere,
even sailing West, West across the sea
to America, where the sun goes every night.

Documentary

So dark it was they almost sat on someone.
"Hey!" Yiddish apologies. Seats! So dark
you couldn't see your– Ai! Blindness! White
blindness, a wall of white. My grandmother hid
her eyes as from an angel. This was worth
two trolleys? Blind in dark, blind in light, better
on the street, a car might hit you but you'd see it.
Their eyes adapted. Shadows evolved, creeping
through white like animals. A fury of snow.
Blizzard, yes. Sky was snow, snow ground, ground sky.
Snow they knew, but such a world of snow!
A puzzle. Zaydee'd ask around at shul.

From the kayak out pop the family
flashing five smiles for the cranking camera.
Hugging a Victrola, Nanook laughs,
searching for the miniature crooner.
Sober, logical white dry goods merchant
holds up record, points to groove. Nanook laughs.
My grandfather gripped his armrests; he shouldn't
rush up to the screen and peek behind.

He builds his igloo like a pastry chef,
cutting, stacking blocks of snow and smoothing
it all with frosting. Zaydee, a tailor,
thrilled at his dexterity and his knife
of walrus bone. A thick ice slab window
like a jewel admits the precious light.

Starving, delirious at landing salmon,
Nanook sinks his grin in the fish's brain.
Black blood runs down his jaw and down the salmon.
Another. Sinks grin. Black blood. The walrus hunt:
chunks of fresh flesh burn his face black. No cooking.
No blessing. My grandfather watched to warn
grandmother when to raise her eyes from her lap.

The blizzard reawakens. Dogs fight, fanging,
howling. The storm howls too, like silent wolves.
As night drops, the family find an igloo
abandoned for the transport through white zero.
Huddled inside, they haul off sealskins, baring
gray gleaming skin, gray gleaming naked breasts,
and then a second, smaller pair (the daughter?),
my grandparents' faces burning with blood.
Nanook sleeps a million miles away.
All dark once more. Then lights. What golden idols!

Gold elephants, peacocks on every pillar,
gold women lay with lions and unicorns:
a roof that burned. Was this the face of God?
An usher mesmerized them into the aisle,
hurried them up and out to the street
where snow piled up in lean forms, like salt men
and women. Driven from the royal hall,
they watched cars stall. Horses stamped. People fell.
They picked their way home, each step crunching cold
until their feet felt no tingle of blood.
But that they expected. That they understood.

Welcome to the Family

When my mother's zayda died
the Brooklyn gravediggers
struck. The corpse lay ready,
the planks and pegs

of his plain pine box
required rot, so my uncles
shed dark suitcoats, hefted mattocks,
grappled among graves with shovels

and built a hole. The men
wore hats and their beards shook
fruitless sweat into the ground.
They knew they had to work:

time and law demanded it.
My father, the youngest, wore
his new suit
he'd saved for for almost a year.

Earth stuck and crusted it. The sun
dampened them all, made their
flesh heavy, redolent, rotten,
the hottest August on the books. My mother

not yet round but cousins buzzed
like workers round the queen.
Her skin flamed, her eyes glazed,
she woke up in the limousine,

her sister holding a compress
to her head. Till six feet
my father shoveled. He faced a face
of dark earth and felt made of sweat

and the cool ground, crawling with vermin,
delighted him. He stood out of
the sun, at rest, his blue suit brown,
then labored up ladder out of

the grave to make a pallbearer
lurching under the coffin, shaking,
making it disappear.
After dragging earth out, kicking

it back in was a blessing. Cool
grass grew next year on the grave
when the living met to unveil
his stone. I made the rabbi laugh:

gurgling and babbling, I puked

on my father's new suit, but I can't remember.

My goggle-eyes couldn't focus

the carved Hebrew letters of my name.

The Trophy

In 1938, between the newsreel
and the main feature at the Paramount
my grandfather's harmonica transcription
of *Bei Mir Bist du Schoen* while he tapdanced
took the runner-up amateur night trophy.
Now, between the loving cup and a cut-
glass silver-lidded dish (a reliquary
for raspberry jellies), propped, cushioned, the Star
of India: his feet, swollen like Popeye's,
ballooning like Fats' "pedal extremities."

Carrying him through all extremes of Brooklyn—
my grandmother shouting but he would make
in the blizzard's teeth the last man in the minyan—
they would no longer walk him by the way.
I watched my father fetch the razor and fight
his father's week-old iron stubble. Zaydee
couldn't walk. He couldn't lift his arms.

He used to gallop me on his knee, one hand
reining my waist, the other tapping hoofbeats
on his jaundiced plastic cigarette box,
and he'd whistle the birds and chirp the crickets out
on the Brooklyn prairie at night. I hadn't

seen him for months. In a voice I couldn't
hear, he made my father promise this time
to stay at home. I think he knew Dad
lied. My grandfather's face glowed yellow as
a caution sign. When I would walk with him
we'd wait for years for every car to pass
so we could cross. When the doctor gave him
three months, he wrote his will and died that week.

My Grandmother in the Home

The blue lounge sofa stank of disinfectant.
I'd brought a bunch of iris but forgot
to give them to her, and clutched their damp wrapper
all my stay. And if her quavery hands
had welcomed them? *Oh, flowers*, she might think,
but wouldn't think to say a word.

I closed my eyes, and she sat at the table
in her kitchen, with a tall glass of tea,
reading Bashevis Singer in the *Forward*–
"That man," she'd laugh, "a sewer for a mind"–
or toting up the dollars in the black
book Zaydee never understood.

And if she wrenched the flowers from my hand,
and if she said a word, it'd be *Are you
my son?* or *I must find my mother*. I missed
her searching, later, comatose, curled up.
Even now she blinked at the strange framed faces
about her in her room. I don't

think I ever remembered her so small.
Her dress was simple as a pillowcase.
Her bedspread and sheets were blue, her hair
cut close like a steel bonnet. She kept
her hands folded in her lap as she stared
out past the door, awaiting visitors
who wouldn't arrive.

Behind the Door

The voices from the other side grew
abstract and unintelligible, not
our mother and our father. Dad would shut
the door to our room, but before the click throw
a kiss we'd catch, giggly with vertigo
from eavesdropping past supper into night
for the return, a glimpse. Cranking the Beatles
up, we hoped to drown their kitchen opera,
so ludicrous, in such a foreign tongue
its deep booms and high shriekings made us laugh
until fatigue would stop us like a slap.
Jabbing the needle to hear Lennon sing
"You're gonna lose that girl," voice like a cliff
high and sheer, we'd tuck ourselves in and sleep.

Did the Black and White Movies Make My Mother?

Did the black and white movies make my mother
paint her nails black and nix all dates except
guys with cars? Yes! Joan Crawford forced her
to pluck her brows to crescent moons, and
Veronica Lake dragged mother's tress across
one speculative brown eye. Careening through Canarsie
in a Packard or DeSoto, her cheeks hollow,
drawing a Pall Mall's shooting star, she'd glow
at her 4F's futile strategies,
and my grandmother, snoring with worry,
would ascend from her dreams at 4 AM,
flustering in gerbil English at
my yawning mother.

                              Life became a process shot,
the real stuff rolling up front while the rest
receded furiously behind, where she ditched
the family candy store, having fobbed
her shift off on my wallflower aunt, promising
introductions, to snuggle down in the dark,
eyes glazed at duckboards in Normandy.
Where was the damn feature?

                    When the War ended
her serious work began. All those returning GI's! Where
was Mr. Blandings? My father, crisp and slender
in his uniform, a Jewish Sinatra,
was the first unhooked Marine she met.
The last three years his long green limbs had leapt
at all instructions: how pliable they were,
how correspondent to command!

What a scheme! As black and white as her
apartment thirty years later, trembling
like a creamy black and white publicity still–
Bacall, Lamarr, or Ingrid Bergman–a ghost
caught in the corner of a color snapshot.

Grandma's Cooking

Plaster, plaster, slap the soup!
Fall from the ceiling, make it good.
Give it flavor, give it spice.

Times Mom's mother cooked she'd raise
her eyes to heaven as she plopped
platters down. My sister whispered,
"This chicken's got *hair*," and dumped
salt straight from the big kosher box.
My cousin choked down by the quart
her homemade odorless applesauce:
some skin, some seeds, some water. When
she turned her back we'd spoon our helpings
into Arthur's bowl. He'd gag
and ask for more. Once she surprised us—
chopped liver—and we chewed and chewed:
she'd forgot to cook the meat.

She moved about her house as if
some weight would crush her, like the safe
in silent movies. She smelled of mothballs,
sometimes worse. The doctor tried
to diagnose: "Why are you always
sad?"

"I have two lovely daughters.
I have six grandchildren. Sad?
Who is sad?"
                    Nobody asked
about Grandpa, rotund
and silent in his undershirt,
settled like a seal before
the TV set, set to devour
her sclerotic meals, to eclipse
them with indifferent, stubbled lips.
He was built of *Don't's*: "Don't cross
the street, Don't go near–, Don't spend–"
When I finished junior high
he dropped a gold watch in my palm
without a word. I felt its gleam,
its cool Art Deco grace, and thought,
Where did he get this from?
Outliving her eleven years,
he still bitched about
a twenty she once lost.

In the ward's bright lights one young woman
flapped her wings and soliloquized,
while a teenage boy with a scarred
face tongued the air like a lizard.
An older man stared like an owl
and never said a word. All
creatures, predators and prey,
dwelled peaceably atop Mount Sinai.
Grandma struggled around the ward,
every step achieved as hard
as Everest, all uphill.
We watched her slippers slap the floor.

They upped the knob to 6; she buzzed
with fear that blotted out—like static's
sweep across the radio—
all regularly scheduled programs.
It swept and dusted Grandma's soul
and rearranged the furniture.
A man with a beard and monocle
angrily stubbed out his cigar
and turning on his humpbacked aide,
shouted, "Enough! Turn off the juice!
You want to have her dropping dead?
I wash my hands—it's on *your* head."

"Yes, master. Don't beat me. I'll be wise."
The room glowed blue. Straps undone,
Grandma sat up on the table,
bolt upright. Just audible,
as angels once appeared in telescopes:
"Can I go home? Can I go home?"

My grandmother began life simple,
then had simplicity simplified.
If the body is a temple,
how can it not become defiled?
If instead it's a machine
how could she have understood
how loose springs and a broken bed
can grind our dreams to bone?

My grandmother ate Vita herring
and borscht and sour cream from a jar.
I don't believe the soul endures.
It bears enough. It drives the car,
takes out the garbage, laughs, despairs.
It shivers my heart
how Grandma's kindness was tolerated
by all of us, the way you listen
to your host's child mangle Mozart.

You clap. We'd kiss, and eat her cooking.

It was her way of looking

after us, forever longing

for paradise, with grandchildren,

for some shell to crack open

and sing, enfolding her in singing.

My Mother's Studio Apartment

White as God, nothing wood, all glass,
mirrors and chrome. My small mother moves
about adjusting blinds and hanging prints.
Her best friend died three years ago while
Mom was last repainting. The funeral
took place in a mausoleum. The coffin
was jacked up and shoved in like a drawer
to moulder behind a white marble wall.
Mom's stopped dating, entertaining, cooking.
She decorates and redecorates: "Our Pixie's
happy in her modern art museum,"
my sister says. Well, accepting. Looking,
she insists, for a smaller studio,
demanding less of her, moving
into smaller and smaller boxes.

The Planes Came Home to the Airport

Saturday mornings I padded about,
drank some juice, padded about
some more. What went *on* in there?

Later, at last, Dad would come out.
Dad would appear! We'd drive out near
the airport, and park by the highway
below the giant orange Erector-set
lights of the landing runway.

Then came the planes! They shook the air.
Wind slapped my face. Propellors growled
in envy as the new jets howled.
What kept them up there?
The turboprops, handsome and redcomb-tailed,
whistled for joy.
Dad hoisted me up to the sky,
where they came in so big and bullet-nosed
that I could wave to the pilots.
Once one waved back! before he eased
the plane straight down the runway bed.

I asked, once, "Do lots of people fly,
up there?" "Yes, of course," Dad said.

Daddy flew. He went away a lot.
I never woke damp from dreams
of burning runways. I never thought
those people in the planes
were coming anywhere but home.

How We Came to Stand on That Shore

How we came to stand on that shore
I don't know, but in the failing
light whose particles sank in the sea
like diamonds, my father threw
his arm around me and walked me down
the beach. "This place was gorgeous then,"
he said, waving his free arm at
the shuttered mansions and concession
stands. "I loved your mother, then."
Tar and glass cluttered the beach.
A steaming smokestack stuck
in the ocean like a lipsticked
cigarette in a coffee cup.

                        Why
we came to walk on that shore I
don't know except
for him to say, as before, "You
are the best thing I have done."
He'd stopped and stood stopping me.
"I've never told you this." The light
had nearly gone. Waves crept in
like sharkfins, dark against dark.
"When your mother and I vacationed

here, I know that there is where

you got started." I followed

his finger up to the boarded-up

window in the now burned-out hotel.

Good Night

Every night Dad brought me to the casement
and I'd say goodnight to the Empire State Building,
radiant in its raiment and enfolding
me in its watchful spotlights, vigilant
as an angel. "Goodnight. Goodnight, Building." Pliant
in Daddy's grip, my torn, eyeless bear dangling,
I'd curl up, the Empire's steeple guarding
the watchful father and the sleeping infant.

I dream of him, his home by the sea, black
waves attacking and retreating. My back-
yard stream chuckles in summer, boils in winter.
In winter, surf sounds pound his bedroom window;
waking, he sees no light fall on his ocean.
I dream this while my stream rushes on.

Transportations

I grant I never saw a goddess go. . . .

Teaching My Students Prosody

My mistress, when she walks, treads on the ground.

My hands have tried
conducting your eyes to follow feet, tried to lead
you fox-trotting through mysteries of scansion:
"Listen: it's got a good beat."

How can I skate you on this ice
shinier than the glaze upon your eyes,
and get your limbs to pump to organ music
until they can waltz to the pure swing of melody
and sing, sure of it?

Remember
the slowing pulse–
75–72–68–
numbering you to sleep
cradled in arms, a wrist beside your ear;

or the tapping in your chest
when you first knew a lie–
the smashed window or someone's "lost"
watch you stole–was contraband with which you could get away.

And getting away: feeling a heart race
in its bare chest on your bare chest
holding a heart syncopating upon that other,
both fluttering in a timeless quickstep
while, pounding, out in the parlor, the pendulum
tells your nerves each step your mother steps
as she trots home with some new shirts
she's picked out just for you, and the big clock
counts Stop Stop Stop Stop.

And suddenly it's you quickening the click of your
steps to the beat of your
blood, and clutching the shirts you bought for your
child, and
today school gets out early.
(Remember counting, pushing
the tiny body bloodily out
and feeling, at last, relief.)

Stately dance
your daughter up the aisle. Abandon her,
then glide
her in the final waltz that will elide
her from your arms forever.

Pace

the long steps following your father. Approach

the space, and count your pummeling pulse. Confront

the coffin

with spade after spade after spade of dirt

until it eludes your sight, in the only place

counting stops.

Playing Ariel

No man is his own. I'm always drafted
for our community theatricals.
My gumsole shoes, my clothes are out of character.
Any clothes are out of character, but they
can't see me wander round behind their backs,
jingling a string of bells as I cry, curse
and hurl spells in my best countertenor.
Here, onstage, I've paralyzed my wife,
Sebastian. *You fools! I and my fellows
are ministers of fate!* I've frightened them
with banging on an iron thundersheet.
Earlier they fell enchanted with
my celestial music, a wet finger
ringing the rim of a crystal goblet.
I duckwalk again behind them: I must
appear invisible and thereby seem
to be in everywhere at once. Too bad
the plot has gotten out of hand and Prospero
has to go to so much trouble. And yet
each moment I find I hardly inhabit
myself. My hands feel not my own: they carve
the air and fill the vacuums they create.
I feel my body lighten on its feet
as my voice lightens in its throat; listen:
my songs recede from all of us at the silent
speed of light. *Be free and fare thou well.*
And opening my eyes I disappear.

The Rock and Roll Angel

for B. D. Love

Who comes in clouds of make-up and flesh,
haloed in henna, lacquer, trash?
Who descends in garments like a star
and bursts new from the black hole of the bar
in a blinding aura? The angel
explodes in light and sound: fury estranges
us from his human form: his mascaraed
eye sears us all. The Telecaster
bumps his hip like a carved tablet.
Against its blood-red pickguard gleaming liquid,
strings more platinum than platinum shriek,
radiating each voice of the blazing
creation, proclaiming *Sin*.

Take us with you into the world of light!
Our world howls to us, but in your throat
is noise made music: it leaps off the frets'
dazzle and quickens in your larynx.
In the billowing fireball we merely singe;
your wings fan brightness, your silver nerves must change
our blood to thrum with electricity
and rhythm engendered in the midnight city.
Thunder us your unearthly progressions,

braid our frayed, diminished souls in sevenths,
twine them round your fingertips, and point!
Animate these bodies with your Word: *Dance.*

The Invention of English

Standing on the stones, we are struck—not dumb;
I ask for an adze and am handed a hammer.
Tongues stick in the throats of men.
The work wastes. We throw it over.
What folly fastened? I forget.
The air in my ear is only wind:
I suspect it sings, but it is silent as I am.

ic eom

I am at the air's mercy,
and if the trees talk, twined in wind,
I'll listen. O let love fall
and strike me with sense as now
on the stones it stripped me. My house

hus

my house halts me, lame. I cannot
enter, allow as my own a house
where I am the infant among my children.
I step, fearful. My fumbling frights me.
I step again; my son steps toward me.
I slack my jaw and shut it; he smiles
and says, says—silence. My son

bearn

my son, speech struck from his throat
by the fact his father fixes on him.
My heir has lost his hoard of words,
and I embrace the boy, braying *bearn*,
bearn, bearn, obeying an alien will.
I turn, and try to untangle eyes,
but hers hold mine, hushed: my wife

wif

the woman who's waited, wasting
while stone struck stone, ever higher.
She speaks no sentence, no syllable, not
by choice. Her wet cheek gleams. The children stare.
She takes my hand and touches it to her hair.
Is there time to teach ourselves a tongue
to live by, to learn to utter love?
Strangers, we must strip our lives and scratch
in the stutter and spit of brute speech,
the impossible anchor of this English.

George Herbert

Susceptible if not yet tubercular–
    the coughing
and shaking from the pulpit! Who'd blame the hellfire-
    hungry for leaving?–
he held intact his mystic ministry
    like a marriage
and took the role of living reliquary,
    breaking down his cherish-
able bits for sick adults and dying children
    at the outlying
farms, and for his mother, Lady Magdalen,
    also dying.
Sleep called its inviting annunciation:
    to be translated!
But he marched up his vicarage's lane
    where work awaited.

Ink stippled paper, each character a stain,
    a cosmos,
an absurd infinitesimal sign,
    a convoluted chaos.
Words, he knew, could weave a web or set
    a snare,
or spring dark woods to bind him in a thicket,
    torn by thorns of meter.

He wrote as if he bolted from his desk
        (rushed back, replaced his quill)
and wandered out into the English dusk
        where with his soul
he entered hands and feet in the church's chinks
        and started up the wall.
He mounted to the steeple and embraced it,
        then rose on
to the pinnacle where, heart heaving, he rested.
        To the horizon
red trees blazed. The crisp air tasted
        like apples.
He clutched the cross

and felt flesh's straitjacket cleaving.
        He watched dark pass
over land and sky till both were black heaven,
        then swung
legs skyward to the axlebeam till by heels
        he hung.
A breeze, a cough could pluck him like a trumpet.
        Lord, Love,
be thou there with subtle webs we wove:
        snare thy servant.

Redon Discovers Color

On a day blazing with spring,
when Monet's canvas slowly would ignite,
or in the heart of summer, when Seurat
discerned the molecules of massive humans
and set each down, or when, on days like this,
Pissarro nudged the sky toward beige and mauve,
Redon, instead, would set down what he saw.
Intricate networks, shadings, organisms,
all black as nerves, would monstrously evolve.
Examining under the mind's microscope
the organs, cells, and nuclei of a spider
that strode toward him, grotesquely smiling,
of a chimera swimming like a shrimp
with the face of one's consumptive younger brother,
"His monsters," said Pasteur, "are fit to live."
And Mallarmé: "His blacks are royal as purples."

On this grayest day, he woke to color. His flowers
no longer had the faces of new widows,
but stamens, pistils, all their apparatus;
no longer grew half submerged in the sea,
but flourished in, of all places, their vase;
no longer shone white light through black-lined features,
but shook with all the wavelengths of the spectrum,
vibrating, knocking in his cranium

so that unless Redon grabbed hold of canvas
and oils, and bore the bouquet into the world,
they would explode. He told Ambroise Vollard,
who said, "So, you confess a world exists?
You're dying to record it, you admit
to Monet's genius?" "What world?" said Redon.

So he began to paint. Light darkened, quickened
in the studio; the spectrum of grays
from white to black rained on his hand and canvas.
His palette shook with perceivable fragments
of pure light, made objective by the prism
of his mind. Jonquils, iris, daffodils,
nasturtiums, roses bloomed under the brush
in a bouquet that took no flower for truth
but from whose colors, textures, and mingled scents
all biological specimens might learn.
They grew to their full voluptuousness
as light failed and Redon brought brush
with color and color and color to them,
color that would refuse to sleep at night,
always keeping from him mere light of day.

Paley Park, East 53rd Street

As they enter, even the leather teens stop
shoving each other before the sheeting wall
of water shouting *Hush*, that must have carved
over eons this park back from the gutter.
Wrinkled by rock, the spray drives summer out,
springing young honey locusts from the pavement
to filter a sky blue as Italian ices.
A woman in black with Aphrodite ankles
flutters the pages of *Paris-Match*, plucks
from a baggie a pearlescent grape,
and delivers it to her lips. Whistling
a Donizetti aria the green
Parkie tips his cap, sweeps trash, and rearranges
the white wire furniture. Sparrows
permit each other first crack at oranges
and crumbs. One perches on my shoe, blinks
at me, decides to go study the man
practicing origami, folding up
his entire *Daily News*. His tabloid birds
flock round him. At the park's exact center
a Chinese woman sits smiling. From
the street the odd taxi honks like a lost goose,
and truck horns crash through the rush of water
like the opening of the Ninth Symphony.

Hogan's Bar, Galway

My wife draws stares, as if she's crashed a wake.
It's a small, brown, dingy place; a grocery
alcove near the door stocks staples: tea
and cigarettes. Men drink and mutter. The one
to himself in a mac and slicked-back hair
resembles Brando in *Last Tango*, dirtier,
with fewer teeth. He buys us Guinnesses
and asks how we like Ireland. Then we buy
his Smithwicks, and he asks how we like Ireland.

Our admiration grows as we consume.
The young landlord collects the coins, his lips
widening each time, discovering more teeth.
A wool-capped man begins to play a jig
on a cheap tin whistle. Two others dance,
and we all clap time.

Each glass is full of nourishment. A kid
comes, buys a box of cornflakes to the music,
pockets his change and leaves. From the huge kitchen,
through the swinging door, the young landlady
carries her baby, pauses so my wife
can bend to kiss him, strolls behind the bar,
and nurses him while the jig plays on.

Inishmore Cuckoo

A hair sharp of a perfect third the cuckoo
rocks on a fulcrum of music.
I check my watch, the only one
on the island to do so, though it's Sunday
when both the church and pubs must open. Off,
it skews melodiously further off. I can't
tell where it perches: pure sound
that overspreads the island, animates
the outcroppings of rock, inspiring dance,
however slow, in stones, on one of which
it must sit, trees nowhere. The voice
holds the island up out of the sea
that punishes it. No one's to be seen,
all in the church, or pubs, or else in bed,
ticking off the seconds to two notes
that swing up like a melancholy gate
after a rain that falls into the ocean
that surrounds and continues to surround
obstinate rock on which the houses perch,
in which the beds reside, in which the people
huddle, comforted in a mutable world
where it is always now, *and* now, *and* now.

In the Lake

After long twilight and longer night and longest drinking;
after the short sleep when half the brain evaporates
and my hosts grunt every time I wake them
with gasps and heaving from their dreams in their vacation
cottage in this pulsing heart of the Adirondacks;
after being stared down and scolded, again, by the white moon;
after watching, huddled on the porch and shaking in a sweat,
how the blackness blues, jabbing at my eyes, growing toward dawn:
hungover I overlook the lake. It throbs
so the trees above bow like ancient heads, and the others, in
the lake, rise, airlessly; but no,
all's still; light grows still, but the brain beats,
tunneling then widening the field of view, these pines,
this plane unbroken by limbs, rudder, or wake,
all pulsing with the head's pain, gasping with the blood.

Water! The nerves and cortex wither like a sponge, curling,
crumbling, wanting water. Here is water–
where? Above are sky, branches, trunks, shore; below,
as solid as above, shore, trunks, branches, sky. Here is no liquid.
Break the pane! crash, dive, drive off
pain, light, air, heat of body and memory of night;
shatter what's past to flounder in a colder element.

I enter the lake and its lower world slicing,
and slipping beneath the surface hear
no noise. Cold. Enveloped, rocked, cold
in the caressing lake, captured from a world of life,
I make a place in the chill that meets
the breathing things above, and suspended
so I touch no solid mud, I see
a translucent gray-green: the edge
of my mother's glass coffee table I would peer
into as an infant when, in love (all before my eyes gray-green)
I gouged the top with a steel toy car
and my first word tumbled from my lips: *apple.*

Opening lips in cold gray-green water I utter
no word and hear no sound but taste a cold, cupric,
apple-like flavor here, where only the light
is solid, like light in glass. If a lover stood
on shore, overlooking the lake, marveling
the mirror where thing meets no thing, with only her inner
ear to tell which sky spread above the trees, which trees' fringes
topped the sky—still she would see the imperfection: to her eye
the lake would not give back all: in a world of light, the dark hole
in the mirror where the silver that glitters and gives back
has worn away, and like the blemish in the perfect surface
lets, unbelievably, light pass through; she would see

what the realm behind the glass refuses ever to return: I.

Get up! go, dive, push upward, work, crash
through the surface, make ripples the sky can't mirror,
love pain, leave pure cold, feel gooseflesh, own to the beating head.
Friends approach the dock, solicitous with soap, shampoo,
and love in a glass of Alka-Seltzer. They will want to know
that I recover. They will want to see
the brightening, reflecting lake before the earliest wake
fractures it for good today, while I, breathing air,
drive off pain the lake can freeze but never heal.

First Hand

This my mean task
Would be as heavy to me as odious, but
The mistress which I serve quickens what's dead
And makes my labors pleasures.

First Hand

From asphalt to dirt road to muck
we drove up to her parents' place
that spring the One-Way Rental truck,
which settled outside the hand's house.
Her father helped in the downpour,
moving our student furniture.

He took an armchair in each hand.
"You'll make a farmer," he said, spat,
and hauled our sofa in. He grinned,
"And if you don't, then piss on it."
He came in again, soaked, and said
nothing, carrying our bed.

My head throbbed. My stomach went sour.
I grabbed the knob, searching for her,
and flung open the crooked door,
but I could only see as far
as stinking cows munching cud
in the rain, knee-deep in mud.

A quart of milk weighs two pounds. A gallon weighs
eight pounds. A fresh cow can give nine or ten
gallons or more, sucked in streams into the Surge
milker hung from a thick steel wire straining
at the wide leather belt it's hooked to, strapped
around the cow's sharp spine and barrelstove belly.
I slap the last tit cup off and grab the tit,
bridal white beneath the muddy, shitted
udder, and squeeze it from the base, jerking
downwards, shooting the last thin stream. I yank
the vacuum hose, heft the round steel Surge
with my right hand, and pull the strap from the cow
with my left. Then I stagger, the sloshing
can listing me all thirty feet, to dump
into the three-legged transfer station milk,
at one hundred-two degrees Fahrenheit
 (thirty-nine degrees Celsius), splashing,
whirlpooling down the station's funnel, sucked
up into the long glass vacuum line, white
as undivided light, racing to fill
the space it constantly pursues, emptying
into the refrigerated bulk tank,
steel, huge, round as the belly of a cow.

I do this fifty-four times every day,
twenty-seven starting 6 AM,
twenty-seven starting 5 PM,
an hour short of perfect, since a cow
must be milked again and again as PM
must always repeat AM, as the night
must parody the day, like it or not.
I'm not sure that I like it, but I'm learning
a labor for love, not for love of labor.

I'm also learning history.

Her father talks *tableaux vivants* while milking:
in the barn, Burr and John Marshall dine,
disputing on the claret, in the cell
where Burr awaits his trial, presided at
by Justice Marshall. Lincoln watches Lee,
gallant in elegant civilian clothes,
slowly walk down the White House steps, alone,
each of them, utterly. So says her father.
One night the power fails. The call goes out
to all hands, former hands, and friends whose hands
have never touched a cow, but wanted to
in secret. Since stripping after machine
milking demands knowing how to milk

by hand, I can do it: fourteen cows,
the maximum, fifty-six tits caressed,
cajoled and jerked down toward the pail that's lugged
the hundred-ten feet past the hollow station,
past the clear glass line, and poured white-hot
into the steadily warming tank, with prayers
the power takes hold before bacteria.
We shut the darkened barn's door and emerge
past ten PM into a night that lights
our faces with the infinite blaze of stars.

Next day the power's back: the milk is saved.
My hands have swollen twice their single size.

Unless I go down town to get it stretched,
she'll never budge the gold band past my knuckle,
not even lubricated with tobacco
spit. It fit when we bought it, before she witched
me into choosing to be overmatched
a season with her father, who has farmed
for twenty-seven years; and though I've learned
to milk with grace, my tractor-driving's botched.

Last Saturday I stayed out mending fence;
her father planted corn across the field;
I felt my Oliver, hooked to a cart, lurch,
and stomped the brakes. The bastards wouldn't hold.
I jumped, and watched the tire roll past my face
before the tractor crashed into a beech.

At night the cows sleep on the hill,
perched at the brim of a green bowl.
They never stir until I trudge
through the barnyard mire, and slog
up the steep bowl's side to call
the cows to morning milking.

Ha-vice. Ha-vice.

I hike up to the first slice
of sun as it begins to rise
above the rim. I rise to greet it.
It keeps rising. Exasperated,
I gulp enough breath to disgrace
the cows into getting walking.

Ha-vice. Ha-vice.

Their tails rise first, their bodies arch
the way a half-ton cat would stretch.
In each cow's face my kind words take,
bringing them down the hill to circle
in the barnyard, round the trough.
The cows walk in for milking.

She comes into the barn to say hello,
her bathrobe white above boots steeped in shit.
Just out of bed, his daughter needs to know
how many eggs and pancakes I will eat,
while I sing softly to the meanest cow,
throwing the strap across, washing each tit.

She pats its flank and pats my back. It kicks,
throws off the milker, cracks me in the legs;
I punch it, almost pulverize my knuckles,
then soothe it, till the milker quietly swags
and the cow calmly munches. Four pancakes,
I tell her, bacon, coffee, juice, four eggs.

'Labor is neither blossoming nor dancing.
Labor is scrubbing, drying, sterilizing
the milkers, station, vacuum line, bulk tank,
shoveling sawdust, shoveling shit, throwing
thirty haybales down narrow chutes, clambering
over the bales in the loft, not even touching
a cow again till evening. Somewhere, watching,
her father's eyes see me in the loft, stumbling
on rafters and loose twine. He is all-seeing,
all-hearing: I know he knows I curse the stink,
the sawdust in my collar, the blisters rising
on hands too sensitive, long spoiled, now stinging.

Inside the empty, dark barn mind grows dark
and travels out the cleaner as it slams
the shit along. All I can do is sing
Sixties junk from the radio, or mutter
what poems I know and haven't yet forgot.
I'm caught in the barn's vacuum, in the middle
between unused-to work and useless babble,
developing my arms, decaying thought.
Her father, in for lunch, scrapes his platter
and slowly utters, in his barnyard slang,
a crystal from his tractor-thoughts, which gleams.
While I am laboring, he is at work.

To break open earth for the sake
of its putting forth glory is something
we pretend not to do. Instead,
we ready the field for corn, and talk,
myself straddling the tractor's fender,
her father guiding the huge plowblades.
As we drive down and into the field,
I watch the furrows of our wake;
he scans the unplowed acreage
and checks the sun. We each perform
our given task. I pursue my saga,
some literary anecdote;
his stare still rises from the field.

I break off, look. A golden eagle
with wings out divides air from air
and drives down the enormous field
made fruitful by its flight.

Although we lie under one roof, my cloak
of sweat and animal odor, like her father's,
lies between us. True, I come in to smiling
eggs or chili patiently simmering,
which fortifies me in my fight, my one-
man trial of darkness. But after shoveling
the calf-pen's murky floor, or scraping off
the loaded milking platforms, I return
to her, painting and wallpapering for the wedding.
Crusted with the worst of earth, I find her
not keenly watching for bears and savages,
her knees propping a shotgun, but stitching,
singing, joining the scraps of her wedding dress.

Here things get repaired in tumult: the clang
of iron pummeled to more useful shapes,
the storm of the blowtorch, the hum and screech
of solder and flux. Things must work. Above
on a rafter, baby swallows in their nest
squeak constantly, although no one listens
except the parents until, when human work
comes to rest, their peeps counterpoint silence.
The swallows, though, keep shooting food to them,
arrowing grubs toward the tiny mouths,
oblivious to noise or none. The chicks
stretch jaws always and pipe their parents home
with gifts from the strange, quiet world outside.

Solstice

The fat sun has stalled in the sky.
It stared me down as I awoke
and feeds on us while we throw hay

off the elevator. Break
can never come. The loft is never
full: though we haul bales and stack

bales all day, we can see the rafter
come no closer to our touch
but hang high overhead as heaven.

The bales keep rolling through the hatch:
we handle them as if they'd flame
beneath sun burning like a match

against our skin. We see steam
rise from us. The day stays, white
and perfect as a bad dream

from which we can't awake. Night
lives in another life, as bright
and far off as a wedding night.

St. Swithin's Day

The seven cleanest cows crowd
the barn door, mooing, anxious
to get aboard. The sky is lead.
It's dawn or dusk. Her father wishes

silently, hard. In '42,
once it started, it didn't stop
till down town they had to row
the old folks out, pulling them up

out of bedrooms into the naked
air. Then they built concrete dikes
on the river. The hay got soaked
and rotted. Neither of us breaks

the quiet milking; we strive
knowing of Swithin's tomb, broken
to bring his bones under the new nave
centuries ago. The worshipers, shaken

and soaked forty days and nights,
watched their clay walls dissolve,
turned their boards into boats,
and saw the grave seal itself.

Now the cows don't low.
We offer work as hard prayer
to Swithin in the blackening sky
lowering on us like despair.

"Deny the plow that furrows land. Division,"
says the priest (her father's eyes glaze over,
blue as his new Sears suit), "must be healed."
On the farm, eight miles from the little church,
from furrows, from seeds, sprouts have grown, and corn,
over knee-high by the Fourth of July,
inches skyward. August will bring harvest,
her father's famous corn roast, ensilage,
and seed to plant in spring furrows, to sprout.

I have left my parents' house to cleave
unto my wife; and we shall be divided
as the hoof of bull or cow be cleft
upon the foot; and we shall cleave together
apart and seek the wholeness in the cleft.

And now the priest, at last, has summoned us.
We vow our utmost private faith aloud
and see the light divide within a golden
circle as I bring it to her finger.

Although I have stolen his golden girl,
her father's features, softer and softer, smile
long, long into the night, until he blasts,
"Hey! Everybody listen!" The hardcore guests,
cousins, friends who've drunk too much to leave,
watch him raise his can of Stroh's, wave
a conductor's hand and tell the hushed chorus
the story of the Filipino whorehouse;
I've heard it half a dozen times in the barn;
but he stops short, just before the punchline,
and wanders into silence. No one cares.
Nieces and nephews practice swilling beers.
Drinking since morning, at last I get dizzy,
and keep drinking, listening to boozy
toasts, kissing cousins; then a strong arm gathers
my shoulders and turns out to be her father's.
Although I'm stopped, the living room still spins.
He talks, though I'm his only audience,
until, flattered and horrified, I see
the subject of his earthy joke is me.

Harvest

The city guests leave
in cars they drive
to town, and give
the darkness, save
stars, burning above,
to us, who have
to learn to thrive
on little but love.

We slowly start
to translate
ourselves, to sort
from gown and shirt
a newer part:
to bring to light
from joy and hurt
a new-joined heart.

Around this bed
let night find
welcome. Let it hide
the walls of this chamber,
the roof of this small house,
the fenced fields full of cows asleep,
and the hills circling like tired animals,
and give us firsthand knowledge of the cows,
the fields, the sleeping world, the Milky Way.

Scattering Bright

For, nor in nothing, nor in things
Extreme and scattering bright can love inhere.

–Donne, "Air and Angels"

Strown Bliss, Scattering Bright

'Look at the lilac litter in the driveway.
You can't stop it; you can't help yourself
remembering its fragrance yesterday,
arching its purple handfuls above

the Dodge, leaking again. You glance from the petals
to my scalp, to the driveway's rainbow of oil,
and I watch you sadden at all this glitter;
you don't need to say it: *Why does it fail?*

Why does it leak away? You know. You know.
In your eyes I can already see autumn,
maples blazing, which like the lilacs lie
underfoot. But what carpets we walk upon!

Toll Road, Winter

Tonight the folded hills resembled you—
dusky with snow, clusters of bare
trees lay like hair, like your dark down.
The sky clung like a blanket to the snow,
and set against its velvet in the air,
like a ripe slice of melon, hung the moon.

What a banquet for my tired eye!
you, the hills, and cantaloupe aloft,
spread out naked as a centerfold
in *Bon Appetit*, as the car radio
squawked, gagged static, and died. Like going deaf,
the Eroica's swelling, unsounded, stilled.

Three Sisters, Late Summer

Faces to the sun,
they lie, bake, and chat
in their flawless skin
about God knows what.

Their chatter
hanging in the ripe
hot air
fragrant as cantaloupe,

they lie all day
and talk–career,
sex, adultery–
drinking beer.

Soles to the sea,
radio to rock,
the afternoon leaks away.
A leaf drifts to one's back.

She plucks it off
as if something dead
and squints at its stiff
astonishing red.

The sun slants
low behind them,
dazzling the ocean's
waves, which would blind them,

except they all stare
from one to the next,
each reciting her share
of intimate text:

one's moving to Greenwich,
one's marrying, she supposes,
one's chucking a marriage
for fresh caresses.

Don't ask why,
as sun starts to set.
Because sand is dry.
Because ocean's wet.

The world's start
came long ago
when a single point
blew

up. Out fell matter.
From that failing began
this perfect banter,
this flawless skin.

Ritual

I stand them in the vase,
one white rose, one red.
"Why two, *always?*" you ask.
"Well . . . Lancaster and York,
the Tudor rose."
And see? As I talk
York perceptibly bows.
Leaves from your notebook
fly off in the breeze.
A speck of silicon
recalls all we forget;
the California coast
may shrug millions off to drown,
or huddled we might watch
bomb or angel burn us blind.
Here: two roses, one of each.

The Vintage

That Gevrey-Chambertin I stole
the year I worked the liquor store,
the year that we got married for
the rest of our lives sits still
in the rack, often the sole bottle,
the vintage we had planned to share
some snowy evening, when we'd stare
across the halo of a candle
years from now, reel back our movie
and laugh at candid photographs,
decades of diapers and grapefruit knives,
in a future ignorant of how we
burned our negatives to black
and left the bottle in the rack.

Returning

Well, the robins have returned,
staccatoing about the lawn,
wrenching worms from underground,
ratcheting a song
whistled like a melodious
patent cure for winter deafness.

Sounds will come. Clocks will jump.
Forsythia will shock the eye,
and lilacs, worse than a ship
carrying a lover away,
will swell your thawing heart
to lodge like a bone in your throat.

And as I watch the crocuses
poking erect from cozy graves,
I remember a kiss above all kisses,
inviting like a glove's
slap across the chin,
before my last turn

from her flickering tongue
to see the lawn all mud and grass
and the robins digging
with mechanistic grace
the creatures they love to pursue
among the roots below.

Awakening

My darling, snow arrived today and piled
up on the thinnest twigs, the lightest branches
like dust collecting on candelabra,
more delicate–don't breathe!–than even your cold
dawn touch those Sunday mornings, before brunches,
the *Times* crossword, and football made us robe.

I don't know why I'm telling you all this,
trudging to the bagel shop alone
while you stretch out in someone else's bed
and wake him with your patented cold kiss.
I'm neither hoping that you telephone
nor praying that a climax knocks you dead,

just that you peek through his venetian blinds
while he's showering and washing off,
and notice the snow's high-piled tracery,
white as sheets, that buries deep as romance
the branch in its unresurrected life
and tests the music of the chickadee.

A Ghost

I caught your ghost
        in an old snapshot where friends
                still drink and talk at our old house.
      It's winter: brown tweeds
              and blue sweaters hide every shirt and blouse,
and the window is blue-iced.

Still everyone smiles in my study,
        mouths open in mid-word;
              the only black and white
        corner of this old world
sits on my desk: the glossy
            8-by-10 portrait
      of your head.

Alone you stare out at me;
        our friends in color neglect
the camera.
        Your indirect direct
            pale gaze
      like a special effect
               next to a live actor
        throws
this world into an otherworldli-
            ness. Otherwise
                you're out of the picture.

The party whirls warmly about
        your face,
                which hovers
                        in its own dimension,
     a place
            forbidden to lovers,
friends, anyone not
                    paying you attention.

Redemption

I'd admired the banana
        as I watched its bold
                brown spots enlarge
                like towns that merge
        into suburbs sprawled
                    even and dark,
                    where people home from work
make kids practice piano;

I'd enjoyed the apples
        exhaling musk
                in cidered
ripples
                like a Chopin prelude
        pressed through dusk.

Love, you've stopped all these
        tragic
                descents. Elderly
bananas and apples
                disappear, re-
        born through your music,
                    leaving deathbeds
                    for cakes and breads,

which I gobble, mystified how
        these fruits I picked and watched rot
              until
I'd think to throw
        them out
now,
            under your hands' skill,
grow
        sweet
        as fruit
              that fall.

A Woman Wades into the Sea

I watch a woman wade
into the sea naked
    as a rose.
        Her long legs diminish,
      then vanish
in the water's
cold hush; I can't see her head.

The sail on the horizon
    may pluck her up:
the captain may listen,
      watching her sip
champagne
    from a plastic cup.

Or she may never arrive
    at that boat;
she may dive
far beneath the wave
      in search of her deep root.
She may find it and live;
    she may float.

Or she may emerge
        far down the shore
where the search
        of my eye and ear
        drowns in the ocean's roar,
past my reach,
past the ticking of my watch.

No chance
        for us! I'll imagine
        she and I tuck in the children,
            light candles and dine
            by roselight, finish the wine,
then dance,

  or I'll wade far out, out where
        the current caresses
        a rose, so deep the watersound ceases,
far,
far from air,
where rainbow fish plant their
        mysterious kisses.

Driving in Fog

And now you're nothing and you're going nowhere.
Trees beckon you, struggling out of the vague
half-dawn and dissolving into the fog
behind you. The road emerges out of nowhere–
all ten yards of it–and runs straight nowhere,
the white lines stuttering, *No dream, just nothing.*
Wheel still feels firm in your hands, but your leg
has gone dead. What in hell are you doing here?

And now on the dim screen floats your lost
father, striding from a far land. Dim your brights.
Where's he gone? He sang that song you loved, you *heard*
it, *yes*. The same tree beckons. The same fencepost
flashes over and over, on each a blackbird
standing sentry in his red epaulets.

About the Author

*J*ay Rogoff was born in Queens, New York, and educated at the University of Pennsylvania and Syracuse University. He won the Washington Prize for *The Cutoff* (Word Works, 1995), his debut book of poetry, set in the world of minor league baseball. His poems have appeared in *The Georgia Review, The Kenyon Review, The Paris Review, The Southern Review,* and many other journals, and his reviews and essays in *The Georgia Review, The Kenyon Review, Salmagundi,* and *Shenandoah,* among others. He lives in Saratoga Springs, New York, with his wife, art historian Penny Jolly, and teaches at Skidmore College.